Rag Cosmology

RAG
COSMOLOGY
Erin Robinsong

BookThug, 2017

FIRST EDITION

Copyright © Erin Robinsong, 2017

The production of this book was made possible through the generous assistance
of the Canada Council for the Arts and the Ontario Arts Council. BookThug also
acknowledges the support of the Government of Canada through the Canada Book
Fund and the Government of Ontario through the Ontario Book Publishing Tax
Credit and the Ontario Book Fund.

 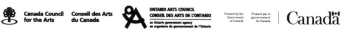

LIBRARY AND ARCHIVES CANADA CATALOGUING IN PUBLICATION

Robinsong, Erin, author
    Rag cosmology / Erin Robinsong.
—First edition.

Poems.
Issued in print and electronic formats.
paperback: ISBN 978-1-77166-314-4
html: ISBN 978-1-77166-315-1
pdf: ISBN 978-1-77166-316-8
kindle: ISBN 978-1-77166-317-5

    I. Title.

PS8635 O266 R34 2017   C811'.6   C2017-900736-X   C2017-900737-8

PRINTED IN CANADA

Souls take pleasure in becoming moist
—HERACLITUS, *Fragments*

CONTENTS

Look at this brown day
look at this brown day
hosted by beauty

I love brown days when the green
leaves have gone back. Down to the future.
As a tree mulches itself. I could bag it away
on the curb on Thursday but I shan't. There are
minerals and gases and the ways that everything
knows. To get to the future. Born for this funeral.
Who will put flowers on a flower's grave?
My anxiety turning
from green to grey
to ash to vapour
to flocked, paisley
fractal, spiral, crenellated
and back to brown

And still it appears
to follow me but is my host –

VIBRATION DESKS

We have information for each other

The first principle of magic is that of correspondence

For five weeks drinking mountain water from the bathroom tap

Looking for the knowledge that is around

Wrapped in mountains emitting clarity while I tramp around
in the potent symbols

I invite the nucleus into this cloud of time and desire

Wearing my favourite new shirt it's silk it's red

Working on my bed

It can be done the old way or everything –

Dogs, vans, lists

And the beautiful black blonde thing of destiny birdsong

Could help you

I've been living without knowing, only knowing

It exists

The tree again, always in pieces of pleasure

What does love do it gives me courage

Green sequins in a squall

I rediscovered no purpose

Alert to the deadly elk mothers

Elements billow and flap

Threw a coin together with space

*

I walk in and I'm already in, don't give me

local limits, I've seen the elements move

through you and through the room

froths, rapids, I don't want this recycled

doom, I want a love weird enough to be a spell

that breaks the spell

who lived in this house and how many worlds?

Just as we know the universe from its folds

as this hand touching me everywhere

I extend my ends to match what is the case –

that I disappear, vanish into this touch

*

Inside its surround

folded in, I'm a fold

of it, I've never left atmospheric

borders I engorge to the point of

enfolded, I'm a pleat, a pore, a breather, a yellow

drape of it

runs through me violetly

dissolving borders to the curve

runs through me nowhere

that isn't here, and I can't crash therefore

the meadow, whoever you are

is a condition of being nowhere

that isn't ejecting only

onwards into here

*

What beings can do to borders

to touch something more

interesting than a border –

maybe this is sex.

My idea is to stay alert

my idea is to go for a walk

to sunset, to darken into privacy

under borders like a life unlike

politics of hot and bleached

oceans and nothing when

in a distracted century I've

taken a walk it's almost

hallucinogenic the things I've seen

I've seen tree bark

I've seen a cloud darkening

I've seen a woman speak into a rectangle

in the generous green *unable*

to receive the advice

that the wildflowers are

unlike a politics of nothing

more than extractive

my interest rate is so low

sexing like a garden

of terminating vegetables

as birds self-deploy

the only surgery available

we had to do ourselves

*

O my friends & associates

night is falling from a singing bird's bright anus

I've lain my head in warm currencies

sporophyllic mouth light in the velvet

of a woman cruising a general doom

and heading left

into the sport of perception

Every cloud everywhere, what that spells

We're so cheap a diamond

a dozen, rehearsals, tears, we had to practice

to become less deadly

And it is

It does not stop, it turns

Does it turn?

Or it does not stop

*

The problem for poets is that poets can do anything

Anything poets want

I don't bleach my asshole

I goldleaf it

2007 marked the end

I left my home, and could not return

                  (oh for my bright black sky)
no eros

like earth, not anywhere

sex a specialty

of here, to have bodies, *to like pulsing well I do*

on this red moving crack in common

feeling language, a symbiotic coin

toward some anterior life

force or spirit, above and blow

passing from finitude to an open whole

it is a force of syntax, of dorsomedial batik upsuck

orbitofrontal cervical stimulations

and there there arose an instance of knowing

the amygdala during a storm / for these citadels of sensation

I burn lilacs in my walk to the transcendentalist shop

*

THE GREEN DESERTS ARE SEEN

SEQUENCES

Spring was coming, it came, it had come

It explodes everywhere, of course, pieces fly

Hors-d'oeuvring around

That the sexual act is in time what the tiger is in space

I also teach a class on folktales for a living

Heartbreak perhaps the best awful thing that can happen to a person

I am reading an anthology of dreams had by French theorists and find myself dubious they can all be true

Faces, before they have decided what to say and how to say it

For instance the dream where Freud – the nanny – intercepts a box of snakes that has arrived in the mail and purées them into a cream sauce

If being lazy creates more work for the lazy person – is the laziness genuine in this case?

A student came up to me last week and said of the Romanian folktale about the dog, that it struck him the cats pursued by this dog were female Jesuses

Though people often do surround themselves with the thing they wish to avoid

Huge hunting birds work out of the trees around my house

In those days, I was panic embodied

I wanted her to know what everyone already knew, that she was majestic

I watched alcohol move through the party loosening it

Then fray and tatter the ends

Tea with butter

I see the clarity of others, clearly

I knew I would always love him, but this was untrue

Of course, I thought, Jesus is both female and plural – why had I not
seen this before?

My life was periodically bookended by dancing; a central bookend

Knowing what I know now

Dancing is evidence of the present and its dimensions

I've been up all night making a powerpoint about the pursuit of happiness

Wearing slouch socks and high heels

Niagara Falls from the air like a black hole

And guestrooms a mark of repleteness –

A whole room for unknowns

They must be wood doves

In the mind

At the split second of coming, the rooster started crowing and we laughed and came and came and laughed

The wood dove tastes more lamb than bird

Stamina of fleurs, stamina of gravity

Eat my ear out

It isn't a self it's a dripping harlequin of hair in a sequin dress without end like the universe or those holes in the ocean

IT IS NO GOOD AND I CONTINUE

To be one's own limit / and to perceive beyond it / is what I do all day

Some kind of fire will begin

That there is a vast interior to time / in bed

Ancient barrier swings

Limit / beyond / day

Who has been to the ocean

Reefs the largest erotica on earth

The cosmos causing things in me / in bed

Personal universes flicker like PRONOUN NOUN VERB VERB
PRONOUN VERB PREP / ADJ PREP VERB, I wake up

Touch extends six inches from the body

A communication occurs between the self and the self, not a split
but a knitting

A walk in the woods with ears

A forest is what seeds can do / in bed

Erotica you could see from space

While I tried to construct answers to match the syntax of the question

It's known. It's all known / in bed

The laws that are criminal

Do you miss the ocean? Of course! The ocean misses me too

Friendship is a round boat

All their faces are planets I have lived on

And how it's difficult to perceiveth

Being so limited with godlike extensions / in bed

To be so limited / and to perceive it / is what I do all day

Overrunneth / night and day

She will come closer, that the energy takes a shape

And the moon, a pervading assistance that is more and less visible
and comes back and gets dark

We can turn out the lights and let seeing into the bed

The vast meshy sea

Aptitude sickness, I spent a lot on nothing much

My side career, my conviction, my male confidence

Always giving the interviewer the answer

It's yours she said, you can have it

CHTHONICS

Green extravagant mind wet and moving

two weeks ago I arrived here

simply to shake in the green plosions

and the tree cloudlike, moves moisture, grows wider

a sphincter in the tree opens my orifices

and I come into time with the shimmering

refuse the obvious depression looped

through a tube of fuckedness, the reefs

the largest living purple on earth

the largest electric green with stripes and tentacled

mouths, swimming vaginas with eyes on earth

violescent sea whips, semiaggressive flower animals

diploria labyrinthiformis, *the chthonic ones, the not-yet finished*

ongoing, abyssal and dreadful ones 24-hours being crushed into

extravagant bunkers for 90 CEOs and their chthonic children even as

the green deserts are seen, fire

is on TV, fire fills the rectangular pulsating apocalypse over the bar

in the restaurant where everyday I eat the kale salad of how real this is

A fire alarm rings deep inside the fire

that *everyone is extremely vulnerable and it's not really in that haha
kind of way*

that *environmental uncertainty can act as imagination for the group*

that *come whenever you want but don't leave*

INTENSE HEAT DEATH AND HAPPINESS

Ecological pressures
internal most

close most deep far up our expensive
moods, intracellular spurtings, secret
constraints spoken here

nothing more than a colour
felt from behind

is to
            need to survive

this lubricated muzzle your diction
glistens in, about

a world of fragile living-on

it's functionally tangled
like a rug
or a dreadlock

its practices it does not say

only colludes as being very close

then swallowed
to the limits / far far

up pleasure, a learning
of the highest civilization

something like a rug
or a dreadlock, the world and I

swallowed
to the limits-in

interpenetrating loops in knots, knotted
as freemarkets

in the succulent
world of fragile

living-in polyrhythms

futures I can only circle
creaturely

Can it be that pleasure makes us objective?

Then this slimming of futures
felt from behind

whose soul demands
this polyrhythmic
little bliss
of going on

I'M WORKING ON IT

Birds could be overheard now

and coming back another way

and part of this is not being free / it's travelling to the far side

and coming back another way

John Cage said something like learning to pay attention and shift states
is addictive

I'm working on it

have you heard about how it takes 10 000 hours

of staring

And after that KC said, you don't need another idea because there are
so many in the ones you already have

Fried oysters again

I do make the present, is a question to ask

and what do I know

about my father

Fried oysters again, on account of our poverty

10 000 hours of staring

at the red weather

Going to the beach with my mother at mid-tide

shucking oysters into a little

bucket of ocean, milky sensitive chaoses for supper

Mature oysters are very large, like a white steak full of guts

I didn't know about our poverty because there was nothing to buy

across the water the pulp mill, the log booms, the barges of woodchips
going by by

but I do

I do make the present, is a question to ask

When I went to parties and would end up onstage naked reading poems

to crowds of brilliant people

The sun
The moon
The stars
The aurora borealis
Bioluminescence

to somehow gather all these into a bucket

to do my program all day and then self destruct

Oysters are bottom-feeders

and I the emoter of the family

could I find a way to ride attention a long way down about 3 mm

Raw oysters for lunch my mother tried to tell me were considered
a delicacy

this seemed to me unlikely

but what did I know

about my mother

it is everywhere, all the time

a group thought on this at a conference the solution was / to make a dance

knowing agency as two-way

the power to affect and the power to be affected

POLYGON

AUTOBIOGRAPHY

5
Oh cloakroom

Hill then hill

Stone steps
in southeasters

Whose nuclear family
fragility

In which oysters
in which again

Therefore bullheads to catch.
Boy George

The Sears catalogue
sells the most beautiful

rocks

14
In that unsearched bag
the river

Above that barn
the hole

On the bus
with those girls

Because bucks of knees
because anywhere

Emits cruelty
whose daylight through

Pines, firs, yews
a fine white steed

Then hill
Then hill

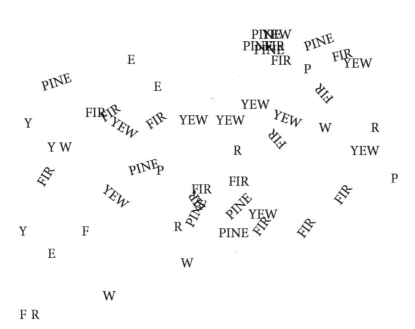

THE WOODS

Pine   fir   yew
    fir, yew

yew knew I
   new   you, knew   aye
    mist hour
       mind

wood
always
long fir
all
  ways
bank in,
would always
   pine   fir
             yew

POLYGON 43576326

The invention of resource goes D   D

fore and aft   WOO SAW   WOO
the entire forest WOU   W   W of
                    D   D   D   D   boats
D WOUL WOO D D unbuilt, landlocked.

WOO   SAW   WOO The inventory
D D doubles when
          sawn in half
WOOO   and   all we
D saw
WOO   became sawn
triply past-tense what we
D   WOUL WOO   WOO
D   D   D beheld
WOO
D   SAW   A drop of pitch hitting
               the centre of a wooden pool
and the years it takes for the rings to
register, to ring out

a record of sawed to dust

in a woodwind. A burlstorm

LIKE EVERYTHING THAT HAS LOST THE
FORMULA FOR STOPPING ITSELF

In habitat hard and high
colourfast and overclean
sipping perishables
from vessels sempiternal –

Forget diamonds. Forget bronze
and cryogenics. Plastics

are   to last, as bodies are
                          to fall apart

                              Bindings and buttons
                              processors and engines
                              discs and doorbells

                                          E   *S*

                  superferries   superglues
tents and toys bust   S
 don't break they

sink
into   *S*
the small   and continents of plastic amass
Waterwings bottles trays syringes airbags action figures

      gather in   *S*   gyres in the sea
E   Duck and   pop. Wow and flutter
          Building an empire in the
     A
                                      S
         bodies   *S*
of everything

BANK OF SOUND

Our banks are tender
our banks for sea
our interest

Our banks
would trust
our bonds
Our banks forgive, our banks

      float

banks are safe
our banks rain
our banks wood
weight
    wood
profit knot   not our bank
our bank would not crack
   hour bonds

would not crack organs, seeds, ore sums
would not sell our cells
for profit
or tender
our sons

THE MIDDLE AGES

TRANSFORMER

As a child I did my banking at the river

and over a period of time deposited

my father's roman coin collection there

fearing for their safety in the sock drawer

which could be robbed or burned.

I could not take this risk

Nor tell him where in the riverbank

they were stowed anymore, and it

was safer this way. Misunderstanding

my intent he took out his metal

detector and once again began

searching. I searched too

for rocks with telltale markings

which I bottled in riverwater

so they would not grow dull

and lose their value as they will

without the river. I was saving up

to pay off debts, so when my mother bade me

not bring any more stones home

I told her of my plan

and she cried, so I never mentioned

it again, but quietly built my empire

depositing what valuables I found

around the house, withdrawing rocks

when the moon said

                    so

DESTROYER

Okay, I said, sure
Or, I said nothing
Why wasn't I the waterfall, the death metal
Why so quiet

Then to have been just blowing apart
Mostly I remember packing 500 matchheads
in tinfoil, soaking a shoelace in gas
wrapping one end in the bundle
and lighting the wick

To be powerless to have been blowing
apart a log, a vase, a section of the forest floor
loosening salt lids, lighting ourselves on fire
had a taste like
come in –

I ate my adolescent plate of shame

We don't measure such kinds of labour
how I, then a young girl, said yes

CURRENCIES

If my tongue is whet

the traffic / moon / moth / mesh
entered my room with the elements
that composed my nightish mornings

by supernatural bread and wild stores then I delight

I made coffee
in the dark, I made it on flames

Burned furniture, applied makeup in bold strokes

am wealth without end

Readied myself to go at dawn
where I could not bring myself to go at noon

Rammed like a moth

anarchy of the most sensuous kind

the western wall, tattered myself
into a powder

Elk-velvet, ambergris, civet gland, orris, estrogen

I learned to be a resource like this

I was hard to remember
hard to count

LOVER /

Unlover, I died
unlover
I died
in the night

all the curtains
fell

open element of the raw
machine, in rags
and colours
destroyed all separation

red tornados I am surrounded

two ears
are   we

your existence
your existence

/ UNLOVER

We took the lover out of its casing

Schlepped it
 through the moonlit grid

Heard thunder talk
  with the third hole in the centre –

Took the lover down to the sea
went in after and saw the gold and white fish –

Rode horses
  horses in bed

My ideas died beside him
dead of common fantasy

In real life militant rain
has worn me down and there's nothing

Lover in the dark dark wind, in the car
who are you, coming home, love, nothing

Once again I have been unstrategic
and received a wild unspendable sky

ASSEMBLY

Through the early morning

a ritual fleet of cloud
row
        white
  wind   North

to find
my loyal fear
not very far from the harbour

with crimson craftsmen
capable of yielding
all your crew

A rough palace
  holds
all possible help
trained

 as leaves and flowers

For the light
of my companions

the smoke
from their voices
assembled

in a secret   fact

– the spring ones, the summer ones

Not persuaded I wished to appear likeable
to burn at suppertime

And who are, where do
is yours, or are you
the words we're making as gifts
to fear

PLACES TO INTERVENE IN A SYSTEM

No one kept watch, except
all of us.
We made human chains we
wrote operas we
conducted interviews and
released the data and started
smoking again, bought up everything
we could just to stop it, it didn't
we found hope anyway
then lost the case, we
lay on our backs and
just floated. We saw 150 species a day
go extinct we
did not want to be people
we were tired of talking we
started marching we said maybe it's
over, we delivered a formal apology to the salmon
did a controversial pregnant photoshoot
in front of a nuclear reactor, all those nice curves
we made page 15 of the New York Times, ok
and delighted in the letters to the editor that said
I was 'going to give my baby cancer' well exactly
then got scared and moved but it was everywhere
we went like my unstable worth rolling

oblongly on pink shadows of information
glamping among facts. Friends came
and were astronomies. Self-deploying
flora volunteered. This morning the sun
of god shone on the chasmogamous violets
and the world continues in great detail.
What shall I do with my information
I'm an animal in an animal in an animal
I'm a *poem of objects that live by magic*
I'm every idea I ever had, I'll just stay here
as a person. I have a photographic mouth

NOCTURNE

      Sleep's

bright

  black

        suit

       a day's march
   to

caves of
         fennel

  signal the
    dark

what do you call them

          behind the bank
         touch that

BLUE HOLE

EMILY

I remember once in a class discussion of Deleuze –

where everything felt possible in his language

asking a question the teacher did not want to deal with

Do you think our bodies are the only way

we get to be here? I was 20, I was a polyrhythmic

rugrat noticing there is nothing that isn't

moving

heat concrete the permissible –

interweave what we can perceive

and what is nonetheless having a day

A writhing endless-ends sort of day

connects us, bodies in time

Bodies in time is an anarchival sport

Dance buys time

I choose

I choose I would sit around

Do you think our bodies are the only way?

And now I get out of understanding and into a blue field, it's white

(it goes by,   spirals   ahead,   collects
here   here   +   here
language   rises   up   all   over
mouthless   a blue hole   just waits)

I read somewhere that we think of death as a taking away of life

but that actually – you die into life

A hole a wave a blue field is your name, but Emily

is a place that doesn't exist

registers continually

in the writhe, the the

the capacity of the environment to assist us.

Kant and Freud are famous for not recommending anything

In a letter in 1993 you sent photographs and news –

How are you doing? I'm okay. Everything here is going fine. I'm coming to visit you forever in 3 weeks. I'm thinking about being a marine biologist, physical therapist, artist and a dealer. On Tuesday I got a new bathing suit. It's all speckled different colours on navy blue. Men are scum! I'm getting a huge CD collection. The cabin that we used to party at used to be really neat until Mark and Heath literally threw everything into the fireplace! They threw the sofa, a mattress, a door, and most of the supporting beams into the blazing flames. I really miss everyone.

In 2008 –

I'm afraid if I die, I would miss everyone and feel isolated by the death and the
quiet

of losing the self I know

MYSTERIOUS ARMPITS (for Eva Hesse)

FRIDAY I dislike the administration   SUN is part of an entity
      Mon morn something's missing   *a cyclops view–*

WEDS– T & I planning together   Weds eve– could not work
      Sat how far can I go   *black rubber*   England
  hardly

Sun– very little sounded so favourable – *proportionate enlargement*
                                      measure
Fri I want clouds politics, papers, a pot of red
               SAT privacy stability permanence
               since you have accepted this
               temporary way of life

Weds buy supplies, drop book in the bath, refuse
(<u>mature</u> outbursts–)

Frid. loneliness vs. togetherness, *vertiginous regularity!*   SUN I love him
horrifically, paralyzed by the warmth

             Mon *frustration of non work*

TUES I can think   The more I work the
more it sprawls

    Thurs weary of my self   not being taken care of

Sat I think I am ineffectual
    creepy, managed   *HOLES wire or–*

Mon *anything whatever any little part*

WEDS eve! more than reasons ! chaos! friendship !   *filter saw dust*

                    Fri (AM) I want to be a man I love

Tuesd. color, flashes very very

          Thurs days pass around me   *complex circularity*
                              Fri *convolution N involution*

SAT Help. Myself?
Myself

SUN the ending can answer the question   *undulation, sinuosity, coil –*

                    Mon *Mrs. Bitch is out for a stroll bitching*

I feel the reasons why

Weds summer transfers energy and friends how to describe –
cordon cincture cestus

          Sun soft and filled with money
                              Friday, *was at Donald's*

STANDING WAVE

water   we ate at the buffet

water   checked my phone

water   climbed a hill after supper

water   smoked

water   the others went to the hot springs

water   spent the evening

water   that this continues

water   and it was orange

water   comes down from the sky to touch you

water   the firefighter crying on tv from too much fire

water   I watched a doe

water   not moving, not far

water   the underverse belongs me further

water   boil advisory for 20 years

water   in Neskantaga

water   and it was orange

water   that the state of Michigan blocked

water   that was corroding car parts

water   they were worried about losing their jobs

water   who is the weather doing me

water   the stroke from below

water   and lead   and pizza

water   for 18 months

water   had detected no lead

water   Sasha Avonna Bell

(ongoing)

MON. AFT

death is for
the hardcore
not really for
everyone
being eaten
shat frozen
then burned
you accompany
yourself
to what
vast appoint.
without your
face all about
a bond with
the universe
going to
cosmic smith-
ereens now
you're vast
grandmother
through
the kitchen
the hospital

a blue car

and othergates

where guesses are

Monday, 3 pm

DOG MILK

CORTES

The mountain told my eye
its sparkling name
and in return I answered
from the ashes

and green
gathered round

and echoed
       along the windy heights

O my friends
            if you are alone
stretch out both brains
and lash together a middle one

thus three way
we waited for the dawn
fresh and rosy-fingered
as the backs of animals

when evening falls
nobody
yet saved his skin

so we ourselves untie
the ship   took places at the oars

and seek again
an island where
with burning clouds
and loyal dark
we soon rouse

SECESSION GARDEN

Turn rivers into crowds.   Turn clouds into crows. Turn crows
into powder. Turn swans
into burgers.   Turn forests into purses   spasms miasma –
      Turn
around in a ruin
into a swan

                  a cyclone
      Turn twelve
in a psychogenic fugue
Sixteen
Thirty-seven turning
ovals in a pool
into something other
than a mother red
brown   silver moth or
tunnels, tubes without exit –
Turn anxiety into a shovel

Or it does not turn
Does it turn?
Or it does not stop

SWANS BEAT POLICE

Fleeced and de-fleed
any forest can be made to march –

Abbreviate rainforest to rainforce
reinforce the levies and divest the trees
of all treason

In the sprawling palace that is nightly hosed down
everyone is sorry
until sunup

Fir and spruce lower their rates
It comes to blows
to blowjobs, to no jobs

or odd jobs, repairs. Unpaid
as everything else in the world

Riverbanks foreclose but the river persists
in giving everything away

 Our hands won't talk to us

Swans beat police with their wings. Forests march
in the streets. Pearls sweat. Gold goes underground
Clouds release tear gas on the crowds
weeping as they work. The egrets send their regrets

And we

who would like to unite, but can only untie
particular wrists, wrest
if possible, gun from mouth, our own
mouth of everything

MEMBERS OF WEATHER

fire weather   roof peeling weather   house   sliding   away
weather   boat down the road weather   Haiyan.weather
crop failure weather   sliding away or hurtling weather drying up
or filling up with weather   falling
ice shelf weather   polar vortex weather   sandy weather
ice cap melting weather   unseasonable disease friendly sandbag
weather   crops washing away weather   snow
in the Sahara   European ski resort closure weather   Katrina
bed bug weather   coral bleaching weather   coffee blight
blackout stressor weather   cultural aggression weather
at all costs wealthier weather   manmade   extreme   wealther
redwoods moving north   weather wall   weather skull
stormshelter weather   wealth weather   island nation flattening
or subsuming weather   male wealth weather   salt in the water
table weather   *are cars as unstoppable as spring*

POSEUR

If from the dressing of trees
came a sound like music but it was not

And you could tell by the way it did not
enter the bodies of things

Unlike real music which doesn't
hesitate

Which walks through walls
and sometimes we become it

Has x-ray glasses and can see
into your briefcase and your clothes

And never says anything but its music
which we sometimes become that's how much it doesn't

Hesitate, does not do borders
like we do

And we know music from this thing that is alike in every way
except it asks

permission that music does not it just comes in
and helps itself to your

thoughts
fiddles with your energies and

leaves
its unasked for surgery half complete

BY WHICH

Flickering gun-shy dark sensations

Illustrious soft machine
Looped, most proximal
Do you even know
what part of you you are?

Chemist programmer waste management prodigy
structural analyst shamanic kinetic engineer
I'm not. My open palms disorganized dreams
wild chemicals

ruin the mood
ruin sunlight lace
boots up and stare at

shapes that
will not assemble or account for this
whipped black chrysalis
uncut and mixed with math
in liquid dendritic branches whirling
orchestra of alert butter

by which you stare at the day resplendent
in your lack of plans your unrhymed
desires free to dabble in doubt
while the virtuoso, the polymath
of you makes way

EROS

is there a plot
well yes, this morning I woke in my rain shelter so happy to be

a loon

the sun coming fullblast in beams
of wood, of light

like thighs

I've been so alone it is the
clearest sound I could find

upon waking I sometimes try to re-enter my dreams
collapsed little theatres packed tight in their skeins

I open them, slit the skins
but then air gets in and that's it

MERL

A pollen pile, a puddle of dew, a spiral stair
as when the island first comes into view
your hands illuminated by blue light and nothing
hundreds of burlap sacks
a waterfall falling forever inside a trenchcoat

Blood streaks the ivories
all cornfields an invitation now
a song
and a jolly dispute about Aristotle's conception of the divine
as when the island first comes into view
in a boat that's sinking

I wear your tooth as a memento
destroyer of 800 dollar shirts
a waterfall falling forever inside a trenchcoat
a song to
all cornfields an invitation now
a lighthouse I'll procure for thee

A small vastness, a floating pavilion
a song to sing
in a boat that's sinking
a lighthouse I'll procure for thee
your hands illuminated by moonlight and nothing

Hundreds of burlap sacks
a song to sing across
all cornfields an invitation now
as when the island first comes into view
a pollen pile, a puddle of dew, a spiral stair
across the gap

BANQUET

Be married you are too much the same.

Tie your rings together, wrap them in blubber

and feed them to a bear. And though you can't be married

you'll be married inside the bear. When the bear dies

you'll be married inside a rotting bear. When only the bones

are left, you'll be married inside clean white arches again.

And though you are too different

and too much the same, and all variations

your greasy rings will be tended

by beasts who don't care

what you are. You are already.

Do you bear this pleasure? You do

THE LATE

It is anticapitalist
to wait for a late person or to
follow a moon's progress bar
folding or being folded into
colours *is the enemy of capitalism*
the inside of a sunset is where the late go
to blink long, their lag composed
of shaved privacies like a budding capitalist
who saved every one or two
dollar coin they ever received
(I am now wishing I had done that)
So much coinage slippage
doesn't make me anticapitalist
not at all I never wait for the late
anticapitalist to blink
or stare long (these are the early
same same) or tattoo eyelids
with a moon's progress bar
building ice hotels used to be such
a capitalist notion not so much now
that there's less and less and less
and less and less and less endless

LATE PRAYER

May our weapons be effective feminine inventions that like life.

May we blow up like weeds, and be medicinal and everywhere.

May the disturbed ground be our pharmacy. May the exhausted

hang out in the beautiful light. May our souls moisten and reveal us.

May our actions be deft as the inhale after a dream of suffocation.

May the oligarchs get enough to eat in their souls.

May we participate in the intelligence we're in.

May we grow into our name. May political harm

be a stench that awakens. May we not be distracted.

Let our joy repeated be power that spreads.

May our wealth be common. May oligarchs come out

of their fortresses and become psychologically well.

May their wealth be returned to the people and places.

May we shift slide rise tilt roll and twist.

May we feel the very large intimacy

And may it assist us.

ETERNAL ATOMIC SUPERFICIAL

A loan in the universe

with multiple endings in the big

family of lace, meadows are revolting

and the army is late. *When women.*

When women. On a self-repairing star

belonging to no one except the sun or the water

with bodies that gush we mustn't lie

about life in the world we have to tell the truth

about the bees whose work is fucking the flowers

not being optional in this world of agates + burrs +

helibore + eggs + money + carnivores + jelly +

ice + space + lovers + organs + nothingness +

oceans + violescent sea whips + limits +

unguents + hot + violet + mottles +

flocks + dogs + circles + splendour +

spores + milk + warnings + bodies +

libraries + opals + flagella + phlox +

borders + mirrors + wool +

mugwort + facts + touch

solutions + dew +

yet +

NOTES

Italicized lines in the book are quotations. In order of appearance:

5   Heraclitus, *The Complete Fragments*, trans. William Harris

9   Tom Waits, "Flower's Grave," *Alice*

13 Anthony Alvarado, *D.I.Y. Magic*, Perigee

13 Fred Moten, *The Feel Trio*, Letter Machine Editions

15 Raqs Media Collective, *Log Book Entry Before the Storm*, raqsmediacollective.net

18 Orlando Reade, "Wildness of the Day: An Essay on Meadows, Rioting, Carnival," *The White Review*

18 "the only surgery available we had to do ourselves" from a text written with Andréa de Keijzer for our performance *This ritual is not an accident*

19 Donna Haraway, *Staying with the Trouble*, Duke University Press

20 Donato Mancini, *Loitersack*, New Star Books

20 After Corina Copp, *The Green Ray*, Ugly Duckling Presse

21 Gertrude Stein, *An Elucidation* (Gertrude Stein: Selections), University of California Press

23 Monique Wittig, *Les Guérillères*, /ubu editions

25 Georges Bataille, *The Accursed Share*, Zone Books

28 Lisa Robertson, "It is no good and I continue," *3 Summers*, Coach House Books

29 After Cecilia Vicuña, interview by Jonathan Skinner, ecopoetics no. 1

30 Donna Haraway, *Staying with the Trouble*, Duke University Press

30 Monique Wittig, *Les Guérillères*, /ubu editions

31 Inger Christensen, *It*, New Directions

31 Florence Uniacke, *Can Get In No Particular Place*

31 Mei-mei Berssenbrugge, *Hello, the Roses*, New Directions

31 Marina Abramovic, performance instruction

32 Monique Wittig, "Intense heat death and happiness," *Les Guérillères*, /ubu editions

32 Claire Colebrook, *Sex After Life*, Open Humanities Press

33 Roland Barthes, *The Pleasure of the Text*, Hill & Wang (FSG)

36 Gilles Deleuze, *Foucault*, trans. Seán Hand, University of Minnesota Press, via Diego Gil

44 Jean Beaudrillard, "Like everything that has lost the formula," *America*, Verso

57 Donella Meadows, "Places to intervene in a system," donellameadows.org

58 Anna Mendelssohn, *Implacable Art*, Salt Publishing

71 Michael Stone, michaelstoneteaching.com

72 Rei Terada, *This Running Water is Death* (film)

73-4 Emily Ellingsen (née Woolley) letters from Tijeras, NM, to Cortes Island, 1993; from Victoria to Toronto, 2008

75–6 "Mysterious armpits" and all italicized lines from Eva Hesse's diaries, Hauser & Worth

79 George Oppen, *New Collected Poems*, New Directions

80 Robin Blaser, *The Holy Forest*, University of California Press

83 Homer, *The Odyssey*, Penguin Classics

87 Bernadette Mayer, *Works & Days*, New Directions

89 Alice Notley, *In the Pines*, Penguin Books

90 Anne Carson, *Decreation*, Vintage Canada

92 Sharon Olds, *The Unswept Room*, Knopf

93 Karl Larsson, *Parrot*, Paraguay Press

94 After seeing WIVES' *Action Movie*, where they invent new weapons

95 "Eternal atomic superficial" was a comment from Hanna Sybille Müller one day in the studio

95 Lisa Robertson, *The Weather*, New Star Books

95 After Coco Bayley, cited by Orlando Reade in "The Wildness of the Day"
   - *It is here that the bees come to fuck the flowers.*

ACKNOWLEDGEMENTS

Immense thanks to Jay MillAr and Hazel Millar at BookThug
for believing in this book and bringing it into the world, and to
Malcolm Sutton for designing this beautiful object. And to Julie
Joosten for shining her vast intelligence upon what was initially a
very different book, helping it through layers and layers of change,
all with the very lightest of touches and armies of generosity.

Some of these poems have previously appeared in *The Capilano
Review; Canadian Xtasy; Regreen: New Canadian Ecological Poetry;
The Goose: A Journal of Literature, Environment & Culture; BafterC
BookThug Poetry Anthology;* and *PRISM International.*

I'm grateful for the support of the Ontario Arts Council, The
Canada Arts Council, and the Banff Centre for the essential time,
space and mentorship they afforded me. Attending the Rhythm
Party at Princeton University in 2014, hosted by Lisa Robertson
and Orlando Reade, also deeply influenced and shifted the course
of this book. The people and notions I spent time with there I will
love forever.

And to my readers, friends and mentors who have all helped shape
this book – Joni Murphy, Aisha Sasha John, Lisa Robertson, angela
rawlings, Sarah Selecky, Nadia Chaney, Helen Guri, and Julie
Joosten again – thank you from the bottom.

Dear friends, collaborators, and artists who continuously inspire
and have supported and egged on this process in so many ways –
Andréa de Keijzer, Jacob Wren, Michael Nardone, Corina Copp
and the Brooklyn poets!, Hanna Sybille Müller, Berkley Brady,
Kathleen Brown, Christi-an Slomka, Barzin Hosseini-Rad, Jessica
Moore, Ronit Jinich, Robert Nichols, Megan Boddy, Gabrielle
Nolan, Christine Gordon, Sachika Kosky, Amélie Deschamps,
Cosmo Sheldrake, Michael Stone, Carina Lof, Ruth Ozeki,

Priya Huffman, Esther Shalev-Gerz, Anna Maclachlan, and Mike Hoolboom, and all my Montréal, Toronto, Victoria, Cortes, and London friends – hugest love and gratitude.

To the poets and thinkers whose lines are threaded (in italics) throughout this book – thank you. Thinking with and from your work has been my ultimate pleasure.

I've been deeply altered, in life and in death, by Emily Ellingsen (née Woolley), Dylan Crichton, Constance Rooke, Charlie Murphy, and my Granny Gannon, who left the world during the writing of this book. Endless love –

For my family – Shivon, Lee and Kaeli Robinsong, Bill Weaver, Patty Loveridge, Jason, Leni and Dov Sussman, Yvonne Kipp, Caz Ratcliffe, my grandmother Muriel Robinson, Alfons, and all my Cortesian family – your support and love is astonishing and core. Special thanks to my mum for the title! And Merlin Sheldrake, Friend with a capital F, whose understanding of the world and its strangenesses is an intimate inspiration.

I am grateful for the land on which I've been able to live, all traditional territories of Indigenous people whose relationship with the land, air and water is a sane way forward in this time of ecological precarity.

And to earth, our most ultimate sponsor –

ABOUT THE AUTHOR

Erin Robinsong is a poet and interdisciplinary artist. Her work has appeared in numerous Canadian journals and anthologies, and onstage at the &NOW Festival of New Writing, The Conference on Ecopoetics, Tangente Danse, and others. With longtime collaborator Andréa de Keijzer, she is featured in Mike Hoolboom's film *We Make Couples*, a Marxist love story. Erin holds an MFA from the University of Guelph, is a recipient of the Irving Layton Award for Poetry, and has been nominated for a KM Hunter Award. She has driven horse carriages, sold knives, and restored books for a living, and is currently a teacher and editor. Originally from Cortes Island, Erin lives between Toronto and Montréal. *Rag Cosmology* is her debut collection.

PHOTO: BERNARDO FERNANDEZ

COLOPHON

Distributed in Canada by the Literary Press Group:
www.lpg.ca

Distributed in the United States by Small Press Distribution:
www.spdbooks.org

Shop online at www.bookthug.ca

Designed by Malcolm Sutton
Edited for the press by Julie Joosten
Copy edited by Ruth Zuchter

Cover image is a chromatogram by chemist Friedlieb Ferdinand
Runge, 1855. Chromatograms are self-forming images, the result
of organic and inorganic compounds combined on filter paper
and exposed to sunlight.

BOOK
PRODUCTION
WAR ECONOMY
STANDARD